HEROES OF THE FAITH

FESTO KIVENGERE

The Man Who
Would Not Hate

JILL BRISCOE

WORD
kids!

WORD PUBLISHING
Dallas · London · Vancouver · Melbourne

THE MAN WHO WOULD NOT HATE

Library of Congress Cataloging-in-Publication Data

Briscoe, Jill.
    The man who would not hate / by Jill Briscoe.
        p.   cm.—(Heroes of the faith)
    Summary: Relates events in the life of the Ugandan
bishop.
    ISBN 0-8499-3309-9
    1. Kivengere, Festo—Juvenile literature.   2. Church
of Uganda—Bishops—Biography—Juvenile literature.
3. Anglican Communion—Uganda—Bishops—
Biography—Juvenile literature. [1. Kivengere,
Festo. 2. Clergy.]   I. Title. II. Series: Heroes of the
faith (Dallas, Tex.)
BX5700.8.Z8K583 1991
283'.092—dc20
[B]   91-21393
                                         CIP
                                         AC

Printed in the United States of America

12349   LBM   987654321

To our grandchildren,
praying that Festo's story
will help you learn that
Jesus will give you the
power to love your enemies.

Contents

Acknowledgments

With thanks to Kappie Griesell for her help in researching the life of Bishop Festo Kivengere, to Jane Wrede for her delightful illustrations of Hark, to Sue Ann Jones for her marvelous job of editing, and to Laura Minchew of Word Publishing for her guidance and support of the project. A special thanks goes to the staff of African Enterprise for their help with this book.

1

Into the Night

In the dark African night, two weary people bounced along in a car at the foot of a tall, black mountain.

"Look out! There's only a path. We're not even on a road anymore," the woman shouted to her husband.

The man and woman were scared. When they turned to look back, their worried eyes seemed to shine with tears.

They could not see the invisible angel riding along with them. Hark the Herald Angel had been sent from heaven. His job was to fill in a few gaps in the record of Christian hero Festo Kivengere. But now, seeing the fear on Festo's face, Hark worried that he had found the wrong person. *This man is*

running for his life. Could he really be a hero?
Hark wondered.

Because he was an angel, Hark could hear
people's thoughts, even when they said nothing out loud. Now he could feel the fear that
wrapped around Festo and his wife, Mera,
like a knotted rope.

But Hark could not help the two people.
He had gone back in time. What he was
seeing had already happened. He could not
change it. He could only watch—and
worry—as he recorded the missing facts of
Festo's story.

"Mera is ill," Hark wrote on his heavenly
notepad. "She has a fever and is growing
weaker. She needs to rest. But she's afraid
the soldiers are following them. And if the
soldiers catch them . . ."

Hark could not bear to write the rest.
President Idi Amin's soldiers already had
killed many Christians in Uganda. Festo's
name was next on their list.

So Festo and Mera were trying to escape
from Uganda, their beautiful homeland.
They would be safe if they could reach
Rwanda, the country next to Uganda. But
to get there, they had to cross the moun-

tains *tonight,* before the soldiers found out they had left.

But maybe the soldiers already know about their escape, Hark worried. *Maybe they are already following. Or perhaps up ahead more soldiers wait to jump out and capture the two nervous travelers.*

It was almost too much for Hark. He was not used to being worried and afraid. After all, there are no such feelings in heaven!

Then Hark realized there was still another problem. Sometimes other narrow paths crossed the trail. He watched as Festo and Mera looked this way, then that way. They turned the car around and tried going another direction. Then they turned around again, bumping and bouncing as the car rumbled over the rocky trails. Sometimes the car bounced right to the edge of the narrow path. Mera thought they were going to fall over the steep side!

They're looking for something, thought Hark. He caught his breath as he realized what it was.

The trail, Hark gasped. *They can't find the right trail to cross the mountains. Festo and Mera are lost!*

3

2

The Briefing

Hark's assignment had begun when C. D., the recording angel, had appeared one day during heavenly choir practice.

"Hark! Hark!" C. D. called out. The heavenly choir had been practicing a lovely hymn of praise for a thousand years. This may seem like a very long time to practice a hymn. But God's clocks in heaven keep different time than ours on earth. A thousand years on earth is like a single day in heaven!

"Hark!" the recording angel called again. Hark heard his name this time. He asked

C. D. what he wanted. C. D. was holding Hark's heavenly backpack, a pair of funny-looking human shoes without toes or heels, and a bottle that said "insect spray."

"You'll need these, Hark," C. D. said cheerfully, helping him into the backpack. It took a few heavenly minutes (about twenty of our years) to get the straps over his wings.

"Where am I going?" Hark sputtered.

"You're going on another earthly assignment," C. D. laughed. "You did very well with the last one. So we decided you should collect some more missing facts for us."

Hark thought about his last trip to earth. That time he had gone to Holland to record the life of Corrie ten Boom.

"Am I going back to Holland?" he asked hopefully.

"No, you're going to Africa this time," C. D. told him. "That's why you need sandals and bug spray. Your feet aren't used to prickly thorns and scorpions underfoot. And no one likes mosquito bites."

"What are thorns and scorpions?" Hark asked with interest. "What's a mosquito?"

"Never mind," C. D. answered. "We'll put

5

A giant scorpion in Africa.

one of the Creator's books about earth in your backpack. You can read all about them on your journey. And here's the heavenly camera. You'll want to take lots of pictures."

"But, but—who?" sputtered Hark.

"Festo Kivengere," C. D. replied. He answered the little angel's question before it was even completed. "He's an African bishop."

"What's a bishop?" Hark wanted to know.

"A bishop is a shepherd. . . ."

"As in sheep?"

"Well, human sheep!"

"Oh! I see," Hark said with delight. "He looks after the King's flock. Sometimes people are like sheep. The bishop is like a shepherd who looks after them."

"That's right," C. D. replied. "Festo has been in heaven since the human year 1988. But there are a few parts of the record we still need to complete. That's your assignment!"

C. D. had pulled out the world globe. He was pointing to a part of Africa called Uganda.

"It's a beautiful place of wide, grassy plains and tall mountains," said C. D. "And there are brown, muddy rivers where the hippos live."

"Hippos?" asked Hark.

"They're animals that live in Africa," said C. D. with a smile. "Many, many amazing creatures live there. You may even see lions, giraffes, monkeys, or elephants. And the birds in Africa are some of the prettiest creatures God ever made."

"Lions?" Hark said, suddenly a little nervous. He remembered the story of Daniel in the lions' den.

"I suggest you pick up a little bit about Festo's early years," C. D. said, changing the subject. "We need to know how he came to be a servant of the King in the first place."

"He must be a *special* servant," Hark said softly. He knew it wasn't often an angel was sent to collect details for the heavenly record. It only happened with heroes or heroines of the faith.

"I'm pleased you chose me," Hark said, smiling. "I'll try to do my best."

"Angels *always* do their best," C. D. replied. "But you'll need to be strong. Some parts of Festo's earthly life were filled with danger."

"What kind of danger?" Hark asked, growing nervous again.

Instead of answering, C. D. halted a fast-moving cloud that was floating past heaven's door. "Hop on this cloud, Hark," he suggested. "You can use it like a heavenly escalator!"

3

Africa

As it neared earth, Hark's cloud suddenly turned into raindrops. Hark quickly jumped off. But he still got quite wet. The rain was really fierce—a storm, in fact, complete with thunder and lightning.

"I thought Africa was a sunny place," Hark muttered to a damp bird that had also been caught in the rain. The bird, a beautiful hornbill, had great black and white wings. He spread them over Hark like an umbrella and told him not to worry.

"The rain will stop as suddenly as it started," he said. "Then the hot African sun will dry you out in no time. But you'll have to watch out for the mosquitoes. They're always looking for a snack."

The hornbill then lifted his wings and flew off. Hark hurried to snap his picture as the bird soared into the sky. He wondered what kind of snack the mosquitoes would be looking for.

A beautiful hornbill.

Hark looked around and saw that he had landed in a field. Cattle were grazing all around him. Young boys were standing nearby tending the calves.

In the distance there were small huts with cone-shaped roofs made of straw. Smoke came out of the top of them.

"That bird was right," Hark gasped. The rain had gone and the hot, steamy ground threw a warm mist over him. "Whew! No wonder those boys aren't wearing many clothes!" he said. He put on his African shoes and walked to the village. The invisible angel looked closely at the people's faces.

"Oh," he exclaimed, "how beautiful!" He thought of the Dutch people he had visited

10

An African village.

in Holland. Their skin had been white. These African people were a lovely shade of brown. Their smooth bodies glistened and their hair was dark and curly.

"The Creator made all humans out of clay," said a voice. It was the hornbill, back again.

"I know," Hark replied. "But I'd forgotten there was such a variety to choose from."

"Oh yes," said the hornbill. "There's brown clay and white clay, red and yellow, too, and all shades in between!"

Delighted with the lovely African people, Hark returned to the pasture outside the village where the boys tended the cattle.

"Festo," said one of the bigger boys, "go on home. It's supper time. I'll take over."

"Why, this is Festo," Hark gasped. "It didn't take long to find him!"

He dug in his backpack. C. D. had packed Hark's notepad that never ran out of paper and his pencil that never needed sharpening. Hark jotted down a few notes. Then he flew to catch up with Festo. He had joined his family for supper. A goat had been killed and cooked. There were sweet potatoes, beans, and bananas, too.

What strange food, Hark thought. *It's not a bit like my*

African children show off a fish they caught.

12

favorite—angel food cake! The family was also eating fresh mangoes, a tasty fruit.

"Festo, eat properly," said his mother. "The grandson of a king knows how to eat his supper!"

Hark was impressed! Festo, he discovered, was the grandson of the last king of a small nation. That little nation had become part of a bigger nation that now was called Uganda.

"But he's not rich like most kings' families," Hark observed. "Why, he spends his time taking care of calves like other boys his age."

Hark soon learned that he had gone back in time to the human year 1931. Festo was twelve years old. That was the year a missionary named Constance Hornby had come to Festo's village. Constance had come from England, thousands of miles away. She had arrived wearing a funny kind of hat called a pith helmet. She told Festo about another king, King Jesus.

Festo had loved the stories Constance told about Jesus. The young boy had welcomed Jesus into his heart. He became a child of

God! Before Constance came, Festo had believed in little spirits that lived in the rocks and rivers. From Constance, Festo learned that God is the great Creator.

"Now he knows he is more than the grandson of an African king. He has become the son of heaven's King," wrote Hark. He was thrilled. He was sure Festo would start to be a hero soon.

But that did not happen. Instead, as Hark flew ahead in time, his joy about Festo would soon turn to sorrow.

4

Revival and Anger

Festo went to church often. And he read his
Bible each day. Later he went away from
home to be educated at a good school.

Hark was very pleased to see that some of
the boys in Festo's school liked to pray—at
five o'clock in the morning! One of the boys
invited Festo to join the prayers. Festo went
along. He enjoyed talking to Jesus early
each day.

But Festo did some things that made
Hark sad. One night Hark watched Festo
break a school rule. "Oh no!" the angel said
out loud. "All the other boys are sleeping,
but Festo is awake. He's creeping out of the
sleeping room to smoke a cigarette!"

The next morning, Festo found it very

hard to wake up in time for the prayer meeting. First he felt tired. Then he felt guilty. But the other boys helped him.

After the prayer meeting, Hark heard Festo say to himself, *If I'm going to follow Jesus, I'd better go to the principal and confess what I've done.*

So Festo told the principal he had broken the school rules. The principal prayed with Festo. Then he agreed to give the boy another chance to obey.[1] Hark was proud of Festo. He was learning to be a hero.

But as Festo got a bit older, he had more trouble being a Christian. He stopped praying. Hark was upset to see that, even though Festo kept going to church, he stopped loving Jesus. Festo turned away from his faith.

One day Hark was amazed to hear Festo tell a friend, "I don't know if I believe in God anymore."

"I don't, either," said the friend.

"If we don't believe in Him, then we don't have to do what He says," suggested Festo.

"You mean the things He tells us in the Bible?"

"Yes," answered Festo.

"Well then, that means we can be as wicked as we like—get drunk, cause trouble. . . ."

"Right," laughed Festo. "Let's do it together."

Hark was horrified. Had he mistaken his assignment? Maybe he had the wrong Festo! But no, this was the right man. He was living in the wrong way, though.

Festo began to live a very bad life. By now he was nineteen years old. He had finished school and had learned to be a teacher. He returned to his home village and became a teacher at the church school there. He had to go to church or he would lose his job. But he didn't want to go. And when he went, he tried not to listen. Festo and another friend began doing bad things together.

Festo had only been home a very short time when he noticed strange things happening. People were singing and dancing everywhere, praising God. They talked about Jesus and sang hymns to Him day and night. It made Festo angry.

"People didn't behave like this when I lived here before," Festo told his friend.

It bothered him to hear songs of praise everywhere he went. He wished people would keep their worship inside the church building.

But church was different now from when Festo was a boy. Back then church was a bit dull! No one wanted to sing the hymns. Everyone was bored—especially the kids! In fact, most of the people in church looked like they had just eaten sour pickles! When the sermon started the kids squirmed and whispered. They hoped it would be over soon.

The grownups were polite in church. But as soon as they got home, they began to shout at each other. When Festo was a boy, church people argued and stole things just like people who didn't go to church. They did not behave at all like children of the King!

"Now, everything has changed," Festo said.

"They call it a revival," his friend answered. "It means 'new life.' People say Jesus has visited our village!"

"How silly," Festo laughed. "Jesus died 2,000 years ago. How could He visit our village now?"

"I don't know. But everyone is saying the revival has changed people," his friend replied. "It has changed the ones who used to have such solemn faces. It's even changed the kids who were bored in church. Now they're full of joy in Jesus. It used to be that people said they were Christians, but they didn't live like Christians. Now all that is different."

"It's wonderful!" Hark wrote happily.

But Festo didn't think it was wonderful.

"Why are all the people singing and dancing in the streets?" he asked his friend in amazement. "They are crazy to behave like this!"

"They are talking about Jesus everywhere!" answered his friend, who was also a school teacher. "You can't stop bumping into people who say they have met Jesus. They insist He has forgiven their sins!"

"That's nonsense," said Festo angrily. "It's all talk—silly talk! I bet they still steal and shout at each other just like they used to."

"Well . . . ," his friend said slowly. "They *are* different! I heard many of the children in school say they had met Jesus. Last week we teachers were amazed when some students returned books they had stolen. They said they know now that it is wrong to steal."

"What?" gasped Festo. "Are you sure?"

"Yes," answered his friend. "Quite sure. Why, even my own brother has changed. You remember how he hated singing hymns in church? Well, now he keeps bursting out in song all over the place! Even when he's in the cow pasture! He is *so* happy, Festo."

"I don't like it," Festo replied with a dark face. "It's all a lot of stupid religious stuff. I don't want to have anything to do with it!"

Hark, being an angel, could clearly read people's minds. He wrote in his report that Festo looked very sure of himself on the outside. But Hark knew he was really quite unhappy.

And Hark was right. Festo laughed and made fun of the joyful Christians. But deep inside, an uneasy feeling was filling his heart.

Festo sensed that something big was about to happen to him.

5

"I've Just Met Jesus!"

"Uncle Festo! Uncle Festo!" called a high, shrill voice. It was Festo's niece. "Come to church with us, please," she begged. Festo's twelve-year-old sister ran up to him, too.

"Please, Festo! It's so exciting, we can't wait to go!"

Festo was amazed. "Why, little sister, you used to squirm and wiggle in church. You wanted to go home as soon as you sat down," he teased. "What has happened to you?"

Without a reply, the little girl took Festo's hand. She pulled him along the path to the church. When they got there it was full. People were even standing along the side and in the doorway. There was a light on their faces and laughter in their eyes. There was so much joy and happiness Festo couldn't believe his eyes or ears.

The girls wanted him to come right to the front of the church.

"I'll sit here on the backseat, thank you," he said.

The service began. *I can leave when I want to,* Festo thought. *I'll wait a few minutes and then go home.*

Suddenly his niece stood up and began to talk.

"Why, what is she doing? She's talking about me," Festo said out loud. He was shocked.

"The Lord has told me that all our prayers for Festo have been answered," his niece told everyone in the church. "He will come to Jesus before this day ends!"

Festo was angry. He ran out of the church. He spent the rest of the day getting drunk. His head was fuzzy when he got on his bicycle to ride home at the end of the day.

"Humans always get dizzy and do silly things when they drink too much alcohol," Hark wrote. He was sad that Festo was so angry. He thought about what Festo's niece had said, that Festo would come to Jesus before the day ended. Watching him weave unsteadily along a dusty path on his bicycle, Hark doubted it was going to happen!

Suddenly Festo's friend came running down the road after him.

"Festo! Stop, stop!" he shouted. Festo fell off his bike he was so surprised. His friend's face was shining with happiness. He looked as if he had just opened all his Christmas presents!

"Festo, I have just met Jesus Christ! I know my sins are forgiven. Please forgive me for all the bad things we did and said together. I will no longer live like that. Jesus has given me something much better."[2]

Hark was so excited about what was happening. "Festo is stunned," he wrote quickly. He followed Festo to his home and into his room. Then Festo fell on his knees and cried out in despair.

"God, if you are there, and if you can do anything for me, then please do it now. If I'm not too far gone . . . help!"[3]

Then Festo saw Jesus clearly. The King of heaven looked at Festo with eyes full of forgiveness. Jesus told Festo how much He loved him.

And Festo's life was changed forever.

Festo was soon rushing through the streets. He stopped everyone he saw. "I've just met Jesus!" he told them. "My sins are forgiven!"[4]

Hark looked at the notes C. D. had given him. He read that this was the message Festo would never stop telling. He would go all over Africa and around the world telling people about God's love and forgiveness.

It was a joyful message of love and hope. But in Uganda, this message had already cost many Christians their lives. And many more were soon to die.

6

The Martyrs

Hark carefully checked the history book C. D. had sent along. He wanted to know how God's Word had come to Uganda. After all, Uganda was quite a way from the place where Jesus had lived on earth. *How long did it take the message to reach Uganda after Jesus sent his disciples to tell the whole world?* Hark wondered.

"Well, it says the first missionaries arrived from England in 1877," Hark said, reading aloud. "These were the two men who first told Kabaka Mutesa, the king of Uganda, about Jesus. He did not become a Christian, but he listened to their teachings. Several others listened, too. And a few years later some of the people were baptized."

Then things got bad, the book said. "When King Mutesa died, his son Mwanga became king. He did not like the Christians. In 1885 he even had some people arrested for believing in Jesus," Hark read. "Three of them were young boys. They ranged in age from eleven to fifteen years old."[5]

Suddenly Hark gasped. The book said the three boys had been killed! "And it was for no other reason except that they loved Jesus."

Hark was stunned. "Now I see," he murmured, "why it can be very dangerous to believe in Jesus. Why, it might even cost you your life!"

Hark was curious. He wanted to know more about these brave young boys who died because they loved Jesus. He decided to go back in time to the year 1885. But first he made sure his heavenly pencil was sharp and his camera was ready.

"Come quickly, Mother! Yusufu has been arrested!" a teenage boy was shouting. "He

26

and two of his friends have been taken away by some soldiers."

"Arrested!" the woman gasped. She reached toward her older son, Yusufu's brother. "What for? What have they done?"

"They are Christians, and the king is trying to stamp out the new faith," her son replied.

The mother rushed from her home to find her son. Hark flew along behind her. Soon they saw crowds of people running along a street. They were headed toward a huge heap of wood that was being set on fire.

"Oh no!" Hark shuddered. He suddenly realized the three boys were going to be burned to death in the flames.

"They are so young," he murmured to himself. "They must be terrified."

No one could see Hark as he moved easily through the people. At the front of the crowd, he was amazed to find the three young boys perfectly calm. They were even singing a song!

Now, remember that Hark was the Herald Angel and a member of the heavenly choir. So any song of praise sent him into a happy spin. But he had never heard a martyr's song before. (Martyrs, Hark knew, are people willing to die for their beliefs.)

Listening to the boys' lovely voices, Hark quickly wrote down the words. His favorite line was, "O that I had wings like the angels'. I would fly away and be with Jesus."[6]

Hark wished he could lend them *his* wings so they could escape the cruel flames.

One of the boys asked a friend to take a message to King Mwanga. "Tell him we aren't afraid of the fire," the boy said. "Soon we will be in heaven. Then we will be safe with Jesus."

Little Yusufu could see his poor mother and father at the edge of the crowd. "Yusufu! Reject Jesus," they shouted. "Then you won't burn in the fire."

His mother began to weep. A lot of other people were crying, too—including Hark.

Even though he was only eleven years old, Yusufu

knew he couldn't reject Jesus. Why, Jesus had died for him!

So the boys died bravely, singing their song.

And then, in the midst of the horror, something wonderful happened.

"I want to become a Christian, too!" cried a man who was watching the boys.

"And I!" came another voice. Hark couldn't believe his angel ears. More voices shouted out their love for Jesus. Forty people came to know Jesus that very day because of the brave way the boys had died.[7]

"The enemy didn't bargain for this," Hark said with a chuckle. He was thinking of how angry Satan must be. "It's as if he tried to put out the fire of faith with a big fan. But instead he has spread the sparks of joy all over the place!"

But the boys would not be the last to die for their faith.

"In the first years of Christianity in Uganda, hundreds of people were killed for believing in Jesus," Hark noted. He was reading again from the history book. "They did not try to save their lives. Like the three brave boys, they were willing to die for Christ."

With a great, sad sigh, Hark put his things into his backpack. Then he flew through time for several years. He arrived in Kampala, Uganda's capital city, in the human year 1972.

He landed right next to a lovely statue. It looked familiar.

"Oh," he said when he recognized it. The statue showed the three boy martyrs. "I'm glad they are honored by the people of Uganda today," Hark said.

Then he noticed a big church across the street. It was being decorated. "It looks like they're going to have a party," Hark said to himself.

He walked into the church. The people were talking happily as they hung flowers and banners for a special church service. Listening to them, Hark learned the name of the smiling man directing the work. He was Archbishop Janani Luwum. *He must be the leader of the church,* Hark decided.

Hark also learned that the church service

was being held to honor another person as a church leader, too.

"I'm so excited that he's being made a bishop," one of the workers said to her friend. They were hanging a banner at the door of the church.

"Yes, he *will* make a wonderful bishop," the other woman replied. "If there's anyone devoted to serving the Lord, it's Festo Kivengere."

7

The Terror Begins

Hark was happy to learn that Festo had married a nice teacher from his home village. Her name was Mera, and Festo loved her very much. Festo was a teacher, too. Wherever he went, he taught children about school subjects. He taught them about Jesus, too.

In 1963, Festo had become a full-time minister.[8] And now, after many years of serving the Lord, he was being made a Christian bishop in Uganda. That meant instead of serving one church in a town, he would serve many churches across the country!

Hark followed Bishop Festo whenever he preached.

"I like being in church," Hark announced one day as he settled into a pew. (No one could hear him, of course.) "Festo is a really good preacher!"

Festo and his wife, Mera.

Festo stood before the people with a wide smile on his face. He was wearing a beautiful purple shirt. "Bishops always wear purple shirts," Hark noted in his report. He liked the color. There was a lot of it in heaven.

Hark noticed a lot of boys and girls sitting in front of him. They were still and alert. Their little faces were turned toward Festo.

"Kids usually wiggle in church," Hark said to himself. "But they are still today!"

Festo told a story about his own childhood. ("Boys and girls always like to hear about when grownups were little," Hark noted with approval.)

"When I was a boy," said Festo, "I used to herd cattle on the wide, open grasslands.

One day the sparks from a cooking fire were carried by the wind. They caught in the long, dry grass the cattle love to eat. In a moment everything was on fire!"

"Oh," whispered a little boy to his friend. "That's scary!"

"Sh-h-h," his sister said, poking him to be quiet.

"Everyone hoped the winds would blow the huge fire away from our huts. The roofs of our buildings were grass. Our homes would have caught fire in a minute, but they were saved. The winds blew the fire away from the village," he said.

"The next day, I went out to look at the grasslands. Everything was burned to the ground. The land looked black and dead," Festo said.

"'Mother,' I cried, 'whatever will happen to our cattle now? There's nothing for them to eat. And the ground looks as if it will never grow grass again,'" he recalled.

"'Wait a bit,' my mother answered. 'The rains will come. Then the grass will grow again, thicker than ever. The plains will turn green, and the cows will eat,'" Festo told the people.

"And she was right," he finished.

Then Festo got very serious. "Dear brothers and sisters, our church is about to be burned by the fires of hatred. But no fire can destroy the seeds of faith. Those who hate Christians may hurt us. But we will be like the grass that grows again, strong and thick, after the fire. The church in Uganda will keep growing, and soon we will be stronger than ever."[9]

Church was over. The people came out looking serious. They knew Festo had been warning them about the dangerous things that were starting to happen.

Uganda's new leader, President Idi Amin Dada, did not like Christians. He was like King Mwanga, who had tried so long ago to end the Christian faith in Uganda. Now the terror was happening again, as it had when King Mwanga's soldiers had burned to death the three Christian boys. This time it was President Amin leading a wave of hatred against those who loved Jesus.

Hark flew to the president's palace to see if he could find out any news. Flying around a corner of the palace, he came face to face with a huge man. Hark had never seen such a big man in all his life! He was even more shocked to realize he had very nearly bumped into President Amin! The giant man seemed to tower over all the other people around him.

First, Hark snapped a quick picture of the president. Then he dug in his heavenly backpack for a heavenly tape measure. He was glad President Amin couldn't see what he was doing. *I don't think he'd take too kindly to my measuring him!* Hark thought.

"He's six-feet, three-inches high, and very big around, too," Hark noted.

Hark's history book said Amin had taken control of Uganda in 1971. At first, everything seemed to go along all right. Things were more at ease in the country than before. But that only lasted a few months! Recently, Amin had told his soldiers they could arrest and execute anyone they thought might cause trouble!

"They don't even have to put them in

prison and give them a trial," Hark said to himself. He was getting really worried. "Amin seems to be very frightened that someone will overthrow him. So he's letting his soldiers do anything they want!"

Hark traveled all over the city to see what was happening. A bird flying along with him said, "Come down to the army's secret huts. You should see all the new guns and bullets they are hiding there."

So Hark went to see them. Sure enough, piles and piles of weapons had been collected. "It must be costing a fortune," the bird said. Hark nodded his head sadly.

"President Amin is getting ready to fight someone," he said to his new friend. "And it doesn't look as though he cares how much money he spends doing it!"

Next, Hark walked along a row of houses. He visited some of them to see if he could learn anything more. Many of the people seemed to be very scared. Hark soon found out why.

"My daddy hasn't come home," a little boy was telling a friend. Big tears rolled down the boy's little black face. "He went to work a whole week ago. But he hasn't come back! Mommy doesn't know where he is. She's looked everywhere. We think the soldiers stole him!"

In house after house, Hark heard the same story. People were disappearing right off the streets in broad daylight. A car would screech to a halt. Then men would jump out and grab someone. After they pushed the person into the car, they would zoom away. No one knew where they went.

It was terrifying. But this was just the beginning.

8

Death in the Stadium

Hark flew quickly ahead in time. C. D. had told him to be sure and visit the human year 1973. That was an important time in Festo's life, and there were gaps in the record.

Hark hoped when he landed he would find the country at ease. "By now the terror has surely ended," Hark said to himself.

But he was wrong.

To start with, there were many different tribes in Uganda. A tribe is like a big family where everyone is an aunt, uncle, cousin, niece, or nephew. It's a group of people who speak the same language. They all wear the same sort of clothes and sing their own kind of songs. They are very proud of their tribe, and sometimes they think it is better than any other tribe!

"That often leads to fights," Hark said loudly. He thought it was a shame that people got proud and fought over their differences. Instead, they should see how interesting their differences were, he decided.

Why, if everyone was the same, how boring that would be! Hark thought.

In the past the tribes had argued over their differences. Sometimes they had been angry with each other. But after a while, the tribal groups among the church people began to say they were sorry to each other. They forgave each other for being proud and thinking their tribe was the best.

"Jesus died for every tribe, not just one," a Christian girl told her friend. "We should not fight. We should love each other— because He told us to!"

But even as the Christians in different tribes began to love and forgive each other, Idi Amin did just the opposite. His soldiers were still tormenting the Christians in Uganda. Many had been sent to jail. Others had simply disappeared.

"People are being arrested, and then they're never seen again," Mera told her husband. "And Festo, Amin has started searching for the church leaders. We are not safe anymore!"

"We are safe in the arms of Jesus," her husband replied.

Festo knew something good was happening, despite the terror. True, it was now quite dangerous to be a Christian in Uganda. But Hark was amazed to learn that many people were inviting Jesus into their lives for the first time. And others who had strayed from God's Word were coming back. Churches were often packed full of people singing praises to the King of heaven. By now more than half the people of Uganda were Christians.

This was not what President Amin had in mind when he started all this trouble, Hark thought happily. *He is trying to wipe out the church. Instead, it's growing stronger and stronger every day!*

Then Amin ordered his soldiers to execute some of the people they had arrested. They were to take the prisoners to their hometowns. The towns' people would be ordered to watch the soldiers shoot the prisoners.

Three of the men were to be shot in a stadium in Kabale, the town where Festo and Mera lived.

"I should go to the president. I should talk to him about what is happening. Maybe he will listen to me," Festo said to Mera. "He thinks we're trying to overthrow his government. We need to convince him we're not."

Now, this was a very brave thing to do! To walk right into the palace and face the cruel president was risky, to say the least. After all, Amin was killing and torturing Christians and other leaders. He might kill Festo, too!

Festo went anyway. He drove to the president's palace in Kampala, with Hark riding nervously in the backseat.

The president greeted Festo warmly. (Hark was surprised by this. And so was Festo!) Then Amin told lies.

"It is all right," he said. "You are quite safe. Yes, some of the soldiers are doing bad things. But I am punishing them when they do. So don't worry about it," he said with a smile.

"Mr. President," Festo said, "I hear you have told everyone in Kabale to come to the big stadium to watch three men be shot. Please let these men live. Forgive them for what they have done."

Hark saw a big scowl on Amin's face. *Oh dear,* Hark thought, *now he's mad.*

Festo wasn't allowed to stay any longer. Sadly, he (and Hark) left the palace and headed home.

"How terrible," said Mera when she heard about it. "You mean thousands of people have to go to the stadium to watch the executions?"

"Amin thinks it will stop people from trying to overthrow him," Festo replied. There was nothing for them to do but what the president demanded. When the day came, they went to the stadium.

Three thousand people were forced to attend the shooting. No one was speaking. Dark fear filled people's hearts. Festo turned to two of his pastor friends.

"Let's see if we can speak to the three men before they are shot," he suggested.

"The soldiers will never let us," replied his friend.

"Well, let's ask anyway," Festo said.

"Please, sir," said Festo approaching the soldier in charge. "I am a minister. I'd like to speak some words of comfort to the three young men before they die."

No one expected the soldier to agree. But to Festo's surprise, he said gruffly, "All right. You can talk to them in the arena just before they are killed!"

Festo began to pray. Hark could hear the quiet prayers (angels can, you know). He wrote them down carefully.

"Please, Lord," prayed Festo, "give me the right words to say to these men."

A truck drove into the arena. The soldiers unloaded the three prisoners in the middle of the stadium. They were in handcuffs. Their feet were chained together. The firing squad stood at attention, their rifles ready.

In the stands, the silent people sat as still as statues. There was a horrible feeling in the air. Festo and his friends walked across the huge arena and came up behind the prisoners.

"Oh, dear Lord Jesus! What shall I say? What shall I say?" Festo said out loud. The three prisoners heard him and turned around to face the church leaders.

"Oh!" gasped Festo when he saw their faces. They seemed so peaceful!

Festo didn't have to say anything. As he approached the prisoners, one of them suddenly thanked Festo for coming! The man told Festo he knew Jesus had forgiven his sins. Then he asked Festo to tell his wife and children he would be waiting for them in heaven. He hoped they would accept Jesus, too, so he could be with them there.

The second man said the same thing. He raised his hands in joy and smiled bravely at Festo. Then the third man said, "I am at peace!"

Festo looked at the wonderful smiles on the men's faces. "Why," he said to his friends, "we need to talk to the soldiers in the firing squad, not to these men!"

Festo explained the prisoners' words to the soldiers. When they heard what Festo said, they were shocked. For a moment, they didn't seem to know what to do!

The three prisoners stood tall, smiling at the huge crowd of people. Then they raised their handcuffed arms and waved. Everyone waved back! People who were near had heard the brave words the prisoners had spoken. They saw the peace of God on the men's faces.

Then the shots rang out, and the three men fell.

Now they're safe in heaven with Jesus, thought Hark, standing beside Festo.

Then everyone went home.[10]

In the days following the shooting, Festo preached to lots of people. They had heard what had happened in the stadium. They were amazed that Christians could face death with such peace and joy. It made them want to be Christians, too!

Even some of the soldiers in the firing squad found Jesus. Boys and girls in the schools wanted to belong to Him, too.

One Sunday, 8,000 people streamed out of their villages. They settled on the grass to hear Festo preach. He told them to ask

Festo preaching on a hillside in Africa.

Jesus to forgive their sins. Many people accepted Jesus into their hearts that day.

Hark couldn't write fast enough. Festo's sermon kept him on his toes. He worked hard to listen and write at the same time. And the humans seemed to hang on Festo's words. They were wonderful words of life and comfort.

"God gives us power to forgive our enemies," Festo told a crowd of people another day. "Some of us think power is force and guns. But God gives us a greater power. It is the power to love. We should forgive our enemies like Jesus loved and forgave His enemies when He was on the cross."

"It's hard to forgive our enemies, Festo," a man called out.

"It *is* hard," Festo agreed. "And it's hard to ask someone else to forgive you, too. But God will give you the power to do it."

"Have you ever asked God to help you do that?" the man in the crowd wanted to know.

"Oh, yes," replied Festo. "Years ago I rode my bicycle fifty miles to see a man I hated!"

"You hated someone?" asked the man, surprised.

"Yes, I did," said Festo. "But I told him Christ had forgiven me. And I asked him to forgive me for hating him so much. I told him I was a Christian now, and I saw him as my brother."

"What happened?" the man wanted to know.

"The man cried," replied Festo. "And so did I. Then we put our arms around each other. I had no weapon—no real gun. But I had used God's gun to shoot hatred dead! That is the best power!"[11]

The president heard about the wonderful meetings Festo was having all over Uganda.

"You must be careful, Bishop," Festo's friends said. "People are disappearing every day. Amin will not like what you are doing, speaking out against the cruel ways of his soldiers and their guns."

"We are safe in the arms of Jesus," Festo kept saying.

Then one day the president decided that people in Uganda could not be Christian anymore.

"But more than half of Uganda's people *are* Christians," gasped Mera when she heard this news. "Is he going to kill more than half of the people in the whole country?"

Festo didn't know the answer.

Then the worst of the terror began. By the time it ended, nearly half a million people in Uganda would be killed by Amin's soldiers. Most of them would be Christians.[12]

By now everyone knew that Archbishop Luwum and Bishop Festo were high on the list of those to be killed!

Some people said Festo was already dead.

9

Charity

Hark wondered about Charity, one of Festo and Mera's four daughters. Charity was a student at the university in Kampala. Hark decided to find her. He wanted to see what Uganda's young people were doing about the awful things that were taking place.

"Well, it's as I thought," Hark said to himself when he arrived. "The students are getting ready to hold a meeting. They're going to protest what's happening. But I don't think President Amin will like it."

"Let's get together and pray," one of the Christian students said to the others. "We can ask God to show us ways to stop the killings."

Seeing them pray, Hark thought of how

Jesus loved all young people. He helped them to be brave and bold. When they came to know the Lord, they served Him with their whole hearts.

Flying around the school grounds, Hark finally found Charity. She was quietly reading her Bible before her class. Hark peeked over her shoulder and read the name on her book. "Charity Kivengere," it said.

"So this is Charity," Hark exclaimed. He was delighted to find her. He had just settled down beside her when one of her friends ran into the room.

"Charity, the other students want to stop going to classes. They're calling it a 'strike.' They say that will show the president how upset we are about what his soldiers are doing," the friend said. "They think if he knows how angry we are, he might listen to reason. Then maybe President Amin will stop the killings."

Before Charity could reply, there was a big noise outside. Hark flew through the window (even though it was closed). He could see that the students had locked the gates of the school. They wanted to keep the soldiers out. But now the army was ramming the gates to get in!

"Look out!" shouted a student watching from a top window. "The soldiers are putting ladders against the walls. They are climbing over to get to the school grounds!"

Sure enough, the rough soldiers were coming over the walls. They rounded up the students who had been protesting. They hit them with the ends of their guns. Then they made them crawl through mud and stones to get to the trucks. The students tried to get away. But 200 of them were shoved into the trucks and taken to a terrible prison.

There were so many students in the trucks they were jammed together. They couldn't even sit down. They were very frightened. "What will the soldiers do to them?" worried Hark. Then he gasped. He had spotted a face he knew.

"Oh no!" he cried. "They're taking Charity!"

At the prison entrance the students had to pass a soldier holding a club with spikes in it. As each young person came through the door, he beat the student with the club. Standing in line, Charity began to pray.

Hark wished he could help Charity. But he knew he was seeing something that had already happened. Hark could not change it. But he stood by Charity, hoping his presence might comfort her. He knew angels were God's messengers, and he was glad he could be here.

Standing close, he heard her talking to Jesus. "Please, Lord, don't let the spikes hit my face," she prayed. As she ran past the guard the club missed her face, but struck her body. The spikes caused deep cuts.

As Hark passed through the door with her, the club swung right through him. He was glad to be an angel so he did not feel the pain! "Let me help you," Charity was saying to a young man. His wounds were even worse than hers. Many of the students were hurt.

They moaned and cried and tried to help each other.

Hark sat sadly against the wall for a moment to record what was happening. He knew several of the students were Christians. One of them suggested that they pray.

"Help us to bear the pain, Jesus," one of them said. "Help us to know Your peace and joy."

"Jesus would forgive His enemies if He were here," said a young man.

"We should, too," said Charity.

"Oh God, forgive the soldier who beat us with the club," prayed the young man Charity was helping. "He doesn't know what he is doing."

"These men can't do anything to us that will keep us from following Jesus," said a bright-eyed girl. She was holding a rough bandage over her wounds from the spiked club.

"That's true," added another. "If we die we'll be with Him in heaven!"

Suddenly, the mood had changed. The crowded, dirty jail became a happy place. It was like the joy that had filled the stadium where the men had praised God as they died. Now, despite their wounds, the students were filled with joy and peace.

Hark couldn't stop adding his voice to the praises (even though no one could hear him).

"Oh yes! Oh yes!" he shouted. "Heaven is so glorious. There is light and joy! And the River of Life streams from the throne of God. And Jesus is there! He waits to welcome you! It is a place where there is no need for doctors because no one is ever sick or hurt. There are no graveyards because no one ever dies. There are no tears because Jesus has wiped them all away! It's—it's . . ."

Hark had been flying quickly about the prison cell as he sang his praises. Suddenly, lost for words, he stopped. Just then, one of the students looked up with a joyful smile. He said he was sure he had just felt the touch of an angel's wings upon his face!

By now, news of the students' arrest had reached the rest of the city. Christians everywhere were praying for the young people. Parents began to wonder if they would ever see their children again. You can imagine how Festo and Mera were praying!

Then, to everyone's delight, God answered their requests. All the students were suddenly released![13]

The Christians who had been in prison were so happy to be free. But they didn't know how long it would last.

"Instead of relaxing or going home, we should get to work. We must spend every minute telling other students about Jesus," they said to each other. "He helped us so much in prison. We must tell everyone how He helps those who come to Him!"

"Charity has brought us such great joy," Festo said when he heard what the students were doing for the Lord. "She loves Jesus so much."

Hark knew that sometimes it's hard for sons and daughters to get as excited about Jesus as their parents are.

"When trouble comes, though," Hark wrote in his report, "young people learn to trust God for themselves. That's good! They begin to pray. Before the trouble, they sometimes just let their parents do it! But when the boys and girls pray, they learn that Jesus answers their prayers, too."

Charity learned that lesson in prison. Festo and Mera were so thankful! They knew they would all need lots of prayers in the hard days ahead.

10

"Kill Them!"

Over the next few months people from Amin's government came to the meetings where Festo spoke. Then it wasn't easy for Festo to speak out against the cruel killings. After all, Amin's people might get very angry and arrest him on the spot!

But Festo knew that Jesus had always spoken out about injustice. The Lord hadn't worried about His own safety, so Festo bravely followed in His steps. He preached against the bad things that were going on.

One day Festo reminded the people that all power comes from God. People who misuse that power will have to answer to God, he said. Everyone knew he was talking about President Amin.

"Some use their power to make themselves rich," Festo said. "And some get fat with it. Then they try to bully other people."

Everyone laughed, even a fat army man sitting in the audience. But Festo's friends were scared. They were afraid the soldiers would grab Festo any minute.[14]

But they didn't. Amin's soldiers had another church leader in mind, first.

"Amin is more nervous than ever," Mera told Festo a few days later. "It's all so unfair. No one is trying to overthrow him. We just want to stop the killings!"

As she spoke, gunfire broke out behind their home.

"Look, Festo!" gasped Mera. "Look at that man. He's just standing in the road, shooting wildly."

"Those poor women and children," exclaimed Festo, watching the terrified people flee. "They're crying and trying to get away from him!"

Hark flew to see what was happening. But something else caught his eye. A few blocks away, some policemen were pulling a man from a building.

"Please don't tie me up!" the man shouted. "I haven't done anything wrong."

But the soldiers took the man away. Hark read the sign on their truck. It said, "State Research Bureau."

What could that mean? Hark wondered, flying along behind the truck. He stopped to pull out his history book. He found the name in the index and quickly flipped to the page. What he read made him shudder. "The State Research Bureau is another name for Amin's secret police," he said. "What will they do to that poor man?"

Hark hurried to catch up with the truck as it roared away. When it arrived at a jail, Hark watched in horror as the police pulled several men from the back of the truck. He knew Amin's soldiers sometimes tortured their prisoners.

When the secret police want to get someone in trouble, they force their captives to say bad things about that person, Hark thought. *Even the bravest people have trouble not giving in. The police torture them until they say what the officers want to hear, even if everyone knows it's a lie!*

As he followed the prisoners to their cells, Hark overheard one of them whispering to the others. "I've heard about this place," he said. "We'll be lucky if we get out alive."

Suddenly they heard cries and moans coming from the other side of the jail. Hark hurried there to find out what was happening. He saw one of the police officers standing over a man who was tied to a chair. The poor man was covered with blood and bruises.

"Oh! They've beaten him until he's hardly breathing," sobbed Hark.

He heard the soldiers ask the man which Christians were hiding guns. The poor man was so badly hurt he could only mumble. "I . . . don't . . . know . . . anyone . . . with guns," he finally answered. Then his head dropped down to his chest.

"Tell us or we will hit you again!" the officer screamed. He raised a thick club above the man's head.

"Please! Don't hit me again! I'll . . . I'll . . . tell you. It's . . . it's . . . Archbishop Luwum! He's hiding the guns." Then the man started to cry.

Hark was stunned. *Archbishop Luwum doesn't have any guns,* he thought. *That poor man tried to be brave. But the soldiers beat him until he said something he knew wasn't true.*

Hark hurried off to the archbishop's house. He arrived in time to hear the dogs barking wildly. Men from the State Research Bureau were breaking down the fence.

"Look out!" shouted Hark (although no one could hear him). The police sprang across the lawn. Eight of them pushed the door wide open. They rushed inside, waving their rifles and shouting.

"We know you are hiding guns in the house. Where are they?"

"There are no guns in this house," Archbishop Luwum answered firmly. The policeman shouted again, "We know they are here. We'll find them ourselves."

"The archbishop's wife was asleep, but she woke up in a hurry," Hark noted. Hark jumped out of the way as the officers burst into the bedroom. They tore the place apart.

"Look under the bed," shouted one.

"Open the closet. Empty the shelves," ordered another.

"Here's a suitcase. Maybe the guns are inside," the first soldier said. He broke open the latch and tore off the lid.

"Look in the children's rooms," one suggested to his companion. "If I were trying to hide guns, I'd hide them there!"

So the soldiers ran into the children's bedroom. The older ones awoke with a great cry when the rough men burst into the room.

"Mother! Father! What's happening?" they asked fearfully. The archbishop put his arms around them and told them not to be afraid.

"What are they looking for?" asked one of the children.

"Guns," his father replied.

"Guns! There are no guns here!"

"I know, my son. But someone has told them there are!"

The soldiers looked at the youngest children, still lying asleep in their beds.

Oh, I hope they don't hurt the children, Hark thought, watching from the landing. The soldiers gazed at the small bodies, sweetly sleeping. Then they turned on their heels and left the room. Hark breathed a huge sigh of relief. So did the archbishop!

63

"They are just looking for an excuse to arrest you," the archbishop's wife said under her breath.

After searching the house, the men left. They had found no guns.[15]

The Christian leaders in the city got together. They were upset about the raid on the archbishop's home. They decided to tell President Amin how badly his soldiers had acted.

Hark was very nervous as he waited outside Amin's office building with the church leaders. *What will Amin say to them?* Hark worried. *What will he do?*

The leaders had to wait outside in the hot African sun all morning and into the afternoon.

"They weren't even given any water," Hark wrote, really concerned. He knew humans needed to drink water, especially when they were in the hot sun. Many soldiers were sent outside to stand guard over them. Then the vice president of Uganda came out and made a speech.

"You have spied on the government," he

began, shouting at the church leaders. "You don't think you have to obey our laws."

That's not true! Hark thought.

"You hid guns to use against us."

And that's not true, either! Hark thought, getting angry.

"What do you soldiers think we should do to them?" the vice president asked, turning to the guards.

Kill them!" shouted the soldiers.

"Why," wrote Hark, "it's like when Pilate brought Jesus before the crowds and they shouted, 'Crucify him! Crucify him!'"

"Let's vote. Who wants them to be shot?" said the vice president. Hark gasped as *all* the soldiers' hands shot up.

The angel was shaking with worry. And he wasn't the only one who was shaking. He heard the soldiers' thoughts. Many of them were scared, too. They didn't want to do such cruel things. But they were afraid of Amin like everyone else.

Hark was relieved that the church leaders were not shot on the spot. Instead, some of them were told to go home. But Festo, the archbishop, and a few others had to stay. They were led into a room where a different official made another angry speech.

Then another man came and told them to leave. But as they were getting up to go, a soldier stopped the archbishop.

"The president wants to see you," the soldier said. Festo stepped forward hurriedly.

"I think one of us should go with the archbishop," Festo said.

"No!" said a soldier rudely, pushing him away.

Festo and a friend sat in their car for two hours. They were waiting for the archbishop to come out. The police guarding the place got angry with them.

"Go home! Now!" they shouted.

"Where is the archbishop?" Festo asked.

"He is still with President Amin."

"We won't go home without him!" Festo replied.

"He'll be home later," the soldier said.

"No! We are waiting for him here," replied Festo.

"I told you to leave!" said the soldier,

pointing his gun at Festo. "Get going!" he shouted.[16]

Festo and his friend drove to the archbishop's house and prayed. Hark stayed behind at the government building. He wanted to look for the archbishop. He searched and searched until he found Uganda's brave church leader.

Archbishop Luwum was dead.[17]

Hark was stunned. *That good, brave man,* he thought as he looked at the archbishop's bloody body. *He did not deserve to die. But he is safe now, with Jesus.*

Then Hark shook with worry. *Would Festo be next?* he wondered.

It wasn't until the next morning that people in the city heard what had happened. The newspaper reported that the archbishop had died in a car wreck! But when his family tried to get his body for burial, the police refused. Everyone knew then he had been murdered and the government was hiding the facts.

A few days later, Hark carefully noted the date. It was February 20 in the human year

1977. More than 4,500 people came to the cathedral for a great service to remember their brave archbishop. Even though Amin had told the people they should not attend, the Christians came anyway. Hark thought this was very brave.

"Our brother has gone to be with Jesus. He is in heaven," said the pastor who led the great service. All the people sang their most loved hymn, "Glory, Glory to the Lamb." Their faces were full of light and joy.

Charity had come to the service with some students. As the funeral ended, she heard some people whispering.

"Maybe Festo will speak now," one said.

"Festo! Festo!" one called out. Others called out his name, too.

But Festo was not there.

"Where's Festo? Where's Festo?" the people chanted.

"Why, there's Charity, Festo's daughter. Let's ask her where he is!" cried a man.

People crowded around the young woman.

"Where's Festo, Charity? Why isn't he here? Is he all right? Did they arrest him?" The questions tumbled off their lips.

Charity looked at their worried faces. She was worried, too.

"I don't know," she told them. "I don't know where he is!"

11

"You're Next"

Hark hurried out of the big church and started looking for Festo and Mera. He looked all over Kampala. But they were not there!

Maybe they've gone back to Kabale, their hometown, Hark decided. He flew there in an instant (even though it was 260 miles away). But Festo and Mera were not there, either! Hark found some neighbors cleaning Festo and Mera's house.

"Oh, we will miss them so! But I hope they escape safely over the mountains," one of the neighbors was whispering to another. "It is such a dangerous trail, and so hard to find. And the nights are so dark!"

"God will protect them," her friend replied. "He will send his angels to show the way."

"They did not want to go," the first woman noted. "They love Uganda. But their church friends urged them to leave this country. They said Festo and Mera could help Uganda more if they were alive than if they were dead!"

The woman talked on with great excitement. As they worked, she told her friend what she had heard the church friends tell Festo the day before. "They reminded Festo that Paul the apostle had escaped from Damascus when his life was in danger. His friends lowered him over the city wall in a basket! And Peter went to another place, too, when the angel let him out of prison," the woman said.[18]

"They begged Festo to leave," she went on. "They told him, 'The soldiers came to your house many times while you were in Kampala. They were looking for you, Festo. Everyone knows you're next.'"

Thinking about what had happened next, the woman's voice became soft. "Festo asked everyone to pray about it," she said. "So they did. After the prayer, Festo decided it was right to try to escape."

Hearing this, Hark realized he had missed an important part of Festo's story.

"And that's the part that's missing from the record," he said, looking at his assignment. So he flew back in time to the day before. Then he set off toward the mountains, looking for Festo and Mera.

He found them that night in a borrowed car, bouncing along the steep, narrow trail at the foot of the mountain. Festo was still wearing the beautiful purple shirt Hark liked so much.

"Oh, Festo, I hope the police didn't see your shirt as we left. They'll know it was you. They'll figure out that we're trying to escape," Mera said a little nervously. "I'm sorry. I can't help but feel scared. It seems so lonely out here. There aren't any signs. And we don't know which way to go! I think we're lost!"

"Surely the trail that crosses the mountains is here somewhere," Festo replied. He looked very worried. "Maybe we've passed it. I'll turn around."

But the path was meant for people, not cars. As Festo swung the car around, it skidded in the loose rocks. It slid to the very edge of the hillside. Mera thought they would plunge over the side! But just in time, the car stopped.

Festo and Mera were scared. But Hark, riding invisibly in the back, smiled as he looked out the window. The neighbor back in Kabale had been right. "Angels are all around us," Hark wrote happily. "They kept the car from sliding off the mountain."

Hark knew the King of heaven sent angels to protect and help Christians. They were also there to welcome the King's children into heaven if it was their time to go. Hark was so happy to be an angel—and to see his friends.

Suddenly Festo became very quiet. "Don't you feel Jesus near us?" he asked. Mera was quiet, too.

"Yes! Jesus is telling me our lives are in His hands," Mera said gently after a bit.

"And He loves us, Mera. Don't forget He loves us," replied Festo. "Jesus was in danger, too. So He knows just how we both feel."

The two tired people—and Hark—rode on in the rattling car. For more than two hours, they looked for the trail. They worried that Amin's soldiers would catch them before they found the right path!

Finally, they noticed a small clearing. Somehow they had missed it as they had bounced back and forth along the hillside. "It's the trail!" Festo cried. "But we're going to have to walk from here, Mera. Do you think you can climb over the mountain?"

"With God's help, Festo," his wife replied. And so they set out over the dark, dangerous path.

Hark worried about them as they climbed. *Mera is so sick,* he thought. *She's afraid the soldiers are behind them. She worries they will hear her coughing.*

But no soldiers appeared.

"God has gone before us," exclaimed Festo as they stopped to rest.

"His angels have cleared the way for you!" Hark added happily, though no one could hear him. "That's what they were doing while you were lost at the bottom of the mountain."

"Mera, do you think you can go on again?" asked Festo after a little while. She nodded, gritting her teeth. They would climb a few minutes. Then they would rest again. And all the time, they were praying.

"Jesus is here. He'll give us strength," Mera panted. And on they would go. "Look out!" cried Festo, catching hold of Mera's hand. "There's a steep dropoff on both sides of us!" Hark went ahead of the two, shining a little of his angel light on the steep path. Mera and Festo thought it was moonlight.

"What do you think is happening to Charity?" worried Festo as they picked their way over the dangerous trail.

"And all the people who helped us escape?" added Mera. "Will they all be safe, Festo?"

"The Lord will help them as He has helped us," Festo replied with confidence.

75

They met the sun at the top of the mountain. What a sunrise it was! The date was Sunday, February 20. In a few hours, the great service for the archbishop would be held far away in Kampala.

Festo and Mera stood on the mountain, looking over the land below. God's creation was bathed in soft mist. The sun, itself, seemed to say, "Welcome Festo and Mera! Welcome to freedom and safety. There is still work for you both to do!"

Going down the other side of the mountains in the daylight was much easier than climbing in the dark. At the bottom, Festo and Mera stopped and smiled at each other.

"We're over the border, Festo!" Mera shouted with joy. Then they began to thank God for the way He had led them out of Uganda.

But their adventure wasn't over. They were in another country, yes. But they still had a long way to go for help.

12

Loving the Enemy

As they walked away from the mountains, Festo and Mera talked about the new life ahead of them.

"What shall we do now?" Mera wanted to know.

"We will have to work hard," Festo replied. "Refugees from Uganda will need our help."

"What we need now is someone to help *us,*" Mera replied with a laugh. "We are refugees, too!"

Hark looked up the word *refugees* in his heavenly dictionary. He learned that it meant "people who had left their own countries because of war or bad things happening there."

On the safe side of the mountain lived a man who owned the only car for miles and miles around. He had set off that morning for the nearest town. Suddenly he remembered something he had forgotten. He turned the car around and headed back home. Then he spotted two very tired, drooping people walking beside the road. One of them was wearing a bright purple shirt.

The man stopped the car. "Who are you?" he asked in amazement. "And where have you come from?"

Festo told him his story. And the man believed him.

"Would you like a ride to town?" the driver asked. "It's a long way to walk—nearly seventy-five miles!"

Festo and Mera were grateful. But they didn't know if they had enough money to pay him.

"Why, I wouldn't take your money! I'll do it for free," the man laughed. So in they climbed.

Their new friend dropped off Festo and Mera at the house of a Christian minister.

The minister had heard about the bad things going on in Uganda. He was saying his morning prayers, asking God to keep Festo safe. That's when he heard a car pull up to his house.

The minister looked out the window. There was Festo in his purple bishop's shirt. He and Mera waved to the minister, and the poor man thought he was dreaming![19] He never expected to see his prayers answered right in his own house!

What joy they shared then! They laughed and cried and marveled at God's love. He had led Festo and Mera safely through the past terrible months.

Seeing them safe at last, Hark's thoughts turned to Uganda. He flew back to find out what was happening there. He saw many people walking, riding, and running toward the country's border.

"Some are crossing swift rivers. Some are walking through the land of wild beasts," Hark wrote.

Just then a guardian angel arrived to help the King's people. "They even passed by lions! But God shut the lions' mouths just like He did in the days of Daniel," Hark told him with a laugh. "I saw it happen."

"Are they escaping to another country where people respect the laws and the laws respect the people?" the guardian angel wanted to know.

"Yes," Hark replied, waving goodbye to his friend.

Then Hark visited some of the homes of Christians who were staying behind. These were families whose husbands and fathers had disappeared or been killed. He looked at the peaceful faces and shining eyes of the women and children. They were sad, of course. It's awfully hard to lose someone you love very much. But Christians know they will see each other again one day. So they were peaceful, too. *The Father's house is a great place for reunions,* Hark thought.

Next, Hark took one more trip back to Rwanda to check on Festo and Mera. He found Festo in a church, praying. Hark turned to a new page in his notebook. He wrote down the prayer. This is how it went:

"Oh, Jesus, see my heart. It is hard and bitter against President Amin. I am angry about the pain and suffering he has caused us. Forgive me for feeling like this. Help me love President Amin and pray for his soul."

Hark watched Festo. For a long time, he thought about Jesus and how He had loved His enemies and died for them. He watched Jesus heal Festo's hard, bitter heart and fill it with love.

Hark remembered what C. D. had told him about Festo's life in the years after this. "He spoke to people all over the world, telling them about God's love," C. D. had said. "And as soon as it was safe, he went back home to Uganda."

C. D. also had told Hark that Idi Amin was forced out of Uganda in 1979. When Festo and Mera went back there, they set right to work. Festo helped start a program to feed the hungry children. He brought in doctors and medicine to keep them healthy. He helped widows and troubled people. And he helped build windmills to bring fresh water to the villages.

Thinking about the work Festo would do, Hark remembered his own work. He quickly finished his report. Then he headed back home to heaven.

13

Heaven's New Song

"Well," said C. D., welcoming Hark. "How did it go?" He was eager to see Hark's report.

"Wonderful!" said Hark. He put away his leather sandals and showed C. D. a little bit of purple cloth.

"What's that?" asked C. D. with interest.

"It's a piece of Bishop Festo's shirt. When he was escaping over the mountain, it snagged on a thorn. I brought it back as a reminder of a wonderful man. He was very brave— a real hero of the King!" Hark replied, smiling.

"You'd better hurry," C. D. said, taking Hark's report. "Choir practice is starting."

Soon C. D. would add Hark's report to the other facts in Festo's record. C. D. already knew this about Festo:

1. He wrote several books about his experiences. One of them was called *I Love Idi Amin.*

2. He had been honored by Christian groups all over the world for his work in helping others and telling them about Jesus.

3. In 1977 he was awarded the International Freedom Prize in Norway.

4. He went all over the world preaching his messages of love and forgiveness.

5. Bishop Festo died May 18, 1988, of leukemia. More than 20,000 people attended the services held in his memory.[20]

"I've got a new song to teach you," said Hark as he arrived at choir practice. "I'll sing it to you. I learned it from Festo and his friends in Uganda."

Then Hark the Herald Angel sang his version of a revival song:

Glory, glory, hallelujah.
Glory, glory to the Lamb,
For His cleansing blood has washed *us*.
Glory, glory to the Lamb!

Listening to Hark's beautiful voice drifting across heaven, C. D. smiled. "That's wonderful Hark," he murmured as he worked. "I'll learn it, too."
And he did.

Bishop Festo Kivengere

References and Notes

References

Some of the information for this story was provided by Dan Wooding, co-author with Ray Barnett of the book *Uganda Holocaust.* Wooding is also a syndicated newspaper columnist, radio commentator, president of Promise Publishing, and founder of ASSIST, an international Christian assistance organization based in Garden Grove, California. In addition, the following books and publications about Bishop Festo Kivengere were used as references.

Notes

1. Bishop Festo Kivengere recounted this anecdote in a sermon titled "Jesus on the Waves," which he delivered 5 November 1980 at the Diocese of Long Island, New York.
2. *Outlook* magazine, Commemorative Issue, Summer 1988, p. 4. Published by African Enterprise, 128 E. Palm St., Monrovia, CA 91016.
3. Bishop Festo Kivengere with Dorothy Smoker, *Revolutionary Love* (Nairobi, Kenya: African Evangelistic Enterprise, 1981), p. 15.
4. Bishop Festo describes the experiences surrounding his spiritual awakening in his book, *Revolutionary Love.* See also *Outlook* magazine, Commemorative Issue, Summer, 1988.
5. For more about the young martyrs, see Dan Wooding and Ray Barnett, *Uganda Holocaust* (Grand Rapids: Zondervan, 1980), pp. 26–27; and Bishop Festo Kivengere, *I Love Idi Amin* (Old Tappan, N.J.: Spire Books, a division of Fleming H. Revell Co., 1977), pp. 10–11.

6. Kivengere, *I Love Idi Amin*, p. 11, and Kivengere, *Revolutionary Love*, p. 82.
7. Kivengere, *I Love Idi Amin*, p. 11, and Wooding and Barnett, *Uganda Holocaust*, p. 27.
8. *Outlook* magazine, Commemorative Issue, Summer 1988, p. 5.
9. Kivengere, *I Love Idi Amin*, 13.
10. The events surrounding the executions in the stadium are described in *Uganda Holocaust*, pp. 65–68. See also *I Love Idi Amin*, pp. 24–26.
11. Kivengere, *Revolutionary Love*, pp. 27–28.
12. "The 'Butcher of Baghdad' Is Defeated, But What About the 'Butcher of Kampala'?" Dan Wooding, "Strategic Times" syndicated column, March 1991.
13. This incident is recounted in *I Love Idi Amin*, pp. 39–40.
14. Kivengere, *I Love Idi Amin*, pp. 44–45.
15. Archbishop Luwum describes the police raid in Festo's book *I Love Idi Amin*, pp. 46–48.
16. Kivengere, *I Love Idi Amin*, 53–54.
17. Wooding, "Strategic Times."
18. See Acts 9:24–25 and 12:17, cited in *I Love Idi Amin*, pp. 57–58.
19. The Kivengeres' escape is described in *Uganda Holocaust*, pp. 117–119, and in *I Love Idi Amin*, pp. 57–59.
20. *Outlook* magazine, Commemorative Issue, Summer 1988, p. 9.

For Further Reading

We recommend these books about the life of Bishop Festo Kivengere. Look for them at your library or bookstore. Publications about Festo also are available from African Enterprise, 128 E. Palm Street, Monrovia, California 91016.

Bishop Festo Kivengere. *I Love Idi Amin.* Old Tappan, N.J.: Spire Books, a division of Fleming H. Revell Co., 1977. (Available from African Enterprise.)

Bishop Festo Kivengere with Dorothy Smoker. *Revolutionary Love.* Nairobi, Kenya: African Evangelistic Enterprise, 1981.

Dan Wooding and Ray Barnett. *Uganda Holocaust.* Grand Rapids: Zondervan, 1980.